A.C. GREEN

Books in the **Today's Heroes** Series

A.C. GREEN

by A.C. Green
with J. C. Webster

ZondervanPublishingHouse
Grand Rapids, Michigan

A Division of HarperCollins*Publishers*

A.C. Green
Copyright © 1995 by Strang Communications

Requests for information should be addressed to:
Zondervan Publishing House
Grand Rapids, Michigan 49530

Green, A.C., 1963–
    A.C. Green / [with] J.C. Webster.
        p. cm. —(Today's heroes)
    Rev. ed. of: Victory.
    ISBN: 0-310-20207-8
    1. Green, A.C., 1963–   —Juvenile literature. 2. Basket-
ball players—United States—Biography—Juvenile litera-
ture. 3. Basketball players—United States—Religious life—
Juvenile literature.   I. Webster, J. C. (Joann Cole)
II. Green, A.C., 1963–   Victory. III. title. IV. Series.
GV884.G73A3 1995
796.323'092—dc20   95-13334
[B]   CIP
                                                   AC

Condensed from Victory *by A.C. Green*
    with J. C. Webster
Illustrations by Win Mumma

Printed in the United States of America
95 96 97 98 99 00 / ❖ LP / 8 7 6 5 4 3 2 1

To the world's greatest parents,
A.C. and Leola,
for your unmovable love and support
and for always being there
to give direction about any decision,
big or small.

Contents

Chronology of Events

October 4, 1963. A.C. Green is born in Portland, Oregon to A.C. and Leola Green.

1981. Benson Polytechnic wins the state championship in basketball. Green is voted *Oregonian's* 1981 All-Metro area player of the year.

August 2, 1981. Green accepts the Lord just weeks before leaving for Oregon State.

1982. Oregon State wins the Pac–10 conference title.

1984. Green selected as Pac–10 Player of the Year as a junior at Oregon State. Oregon wins another Pac–10 conference title.

1985. Green graduates from Oregon State and is drafted by the Los Angeles Lakers.

1987. Green wins his first NBA championship with the Lakers.

1988. The Lakers repeat the NBA championship.

1989. Green forms the A.C. Green Foundation for Youth to help build hope, confidence, and self-esteem in young people. He is named by

NBA coaches to the All-NBA All-Defense second team.

1990. Green is voted to the All-Star game, and Earvin "Magic" Johnson retires from basketball.

September 28, 1993. Green signs on with the Phoenix Suns.

1

Stitches

I was a typical kid. I didn't like getting in trouble but didn't really like following the rules, either. One escapade, however, almost cost me my life.

My cousin Willie was visiting on a bright, warm Sunday afternoon in midsummer. My mom and dad, Leola and A.C., were gone for a few hours, so we thought we could get away with running through the house. My parents' home was a two-story, gray clapboard house in Portland, Oregon. My sister, Faye, was in charge of watching us that day. Faye is five years older than I am. Then comes Lee, four years older, and Steve, a year older. I'm the baby.

"Hey, Junior," Willie said, using my family name, "wanna play tag?"

"Yeah!" I answered. He chased me, and I ran from him.

"Watch out!" I hollered as I threw open the front door and ran through the house.

"You're it!" he said as he tagged me. I chased him out the back door and quickly dragged a chair to prop open the door. We ran out the back door, around the side, onto the porch, then through the front door and back through the house again. Furniture rocked. The floor shook.

"Gotcha!" I screamed.

"Gotcha back! You're it!" he shouted.

"Stop running in the house!" Faye shrieked. But we didn't pay attention. Finally she got tough. As soon as we cleared the back door, she moved the chair, closed the door, and ran to the front to shut that door, too. At that moment, Willie jumped onto the porch, with me hot on his heels, and squeezed through the crack as the door closed.

I was right behind him. I threw out my arm to keep from slamming my face into the door. The glass shattered on impact, leaving a trian-

A.C. Green

gular piece jutting up from the woodwork. That triangle slashed my arm open from wrist to armpit.

"Junior!" Faye screamed.

"Oh, no!" Willie said. "Junior, get up! Stop faking it!"

"Oh, please, someone stop the bleeding!" I cried.

Faye brought towels to sop up the blood. Then she walked me across the street to the Welch's house. Mrs. Welch was a nurse; she wrapped my arm in a sheet while Faye called our parents.

As soon as Mom and Dad arrived, they bundled me into the car, and Dad drove me to the nearest emergency ward, which wasn't equipped for an injury as serious as mine. The staff transferred me to another hospital. They thought I would die because I had lost so much blood.

"Another pint loss could have killed him. You got him here just in time," the doctor said.

The next thing I knew, I was lying in a bed, eating dry eggs and looking at a big bandage covering my arm. When my parents came in and told me I'd be all right, I thought I just lucked out. Years later I realized God's grace had protected me from death that day.

I was in the hospital for a couple of days. At

A.C. Green

first, people brought me gifts. Being the youngest of four, I always had to compete for attention. Now everyone was super nice to me, and I milked it for all it was worth.

When they took off my bandages, my arm was lined with dozens of stitches. Little black threads stuck out everywhere. The wound healed in scabs that looked like a bad case of chicken pox.

When I got home from the hospital, the party was over. Faye, Lee, and Steve smiled on the outside, but they were mad. "We got whippings!" Lee said when Mom and Dad left the room. "You got us in trouble!" Steve accused. It was payback time.

"Bring me a glass of water," Faye would order.

"Change the channel, " Lee demanded.

"Give me that!" Steve said about something I cherished.

As for running in the house, you'd think I would have quit. But once I was back on my feet, I held my left arm steady with my right, and I was off to the races again. I did figure out, however, that being hospitalized was the only way I could avoid discipline. Mom and Dad were loving, devoted parents, but "spare the rod and spoil the child" was a principle they lived out.

2

World-Class Wheelie

My dad loves cars. He was a car detailer and salesman at a Ford dealership until he had an injury when I was a teenager. It left him permanently disabled, though not handicapped. Mom worked thirteen years as a fabric processor at Jantzen sportswear, then changed careers when they closed her division.

Dad didn't have the money to buy us a lot of toys, but when he did purchase something, he always bought quality. He taught us to respect quality and to be responsible for our possessions.

"Here's your bike, all ready to ride," he said as he tightened the last screw. "Ride it carefully, take good care of it, and don't skid those tires!"

All the neighborhood kids loved good bikes. "Look what I got!" I said triumphantly when Dad bought me an orange Craig. I was out the gate on it in a flash.

"Is that a new bike, Junior?" the neighbors asked.

"It sure is," I said proudly. It wasn't a ten-speed or a mountain bike. It was built sort of like a modern-day dirt bike.

"Come on—let's race," Lee said one day. "You go that way, and I'll go this way," he said, "and we'll see who gets home the fastest."

I was younger, not dumber. We both headed for the same shortcut to beat each other. "Look out!" I shouted as his bike bore down on mine, but it was too late. His smile connected with the back of my head.

I walked my bike home with blood gushing out of my skull. For all the blood, it turned out to be a minor injury.

One time we held one of our famous wheelie contests, seeing who could go for a whole block on his back tire.

"Watch this!" I said. Instantly I knew that this was a run for the world championship.

"Go! Go! Go!" everyone screamed as they chased me down the block.

Finally my tire came down, slamming to the ground. My bike frame cracked in half. "Wow, look what I did!" I said.

"What a ride! You hold the record, Junior!" someone said.

"Yeah," I said. "But I broke my bike." I looked in dismay at the shattered orange Craig—my only bike.

I dragged the bike into the garage and carefully arranged the pieces to make them look whole before I faced Dad. But one of my brothers got in the house first and hinted at what had happened.

"I had an accident," I said nonchalantly when I saw Dad inside. "Not too bad."

"Where's the bike, Junior?" Dad asked me.

"I brought it home," I said, maintaining my casual tone.

"Brought it or rode it?" Dad asked.

"It's in the garage," I answered evasively.

He headed for the garage. Holding up the two pieces of the bike, he looked at me. "How'd you do this?" he asked incredulously.

A.C. Green

I had to admit, breaking a bike in two was a pretty unusual feat.

"You're going to have to wait until your birthday to get another one, Junior," he told me sternly.

I didn't see a bike again for a month or more, which seemed like centuries in kid years. Going without a bike was the worst punishment in the world.

3

State Champions

Until high school I was the same height as other kids my age, and baseball was my dominant sport. We played on organized teams, starting young with T-ball. I made it to the All-Stars in Little League. And I was one of my school's top home-run hitters when I got to junior high.

But I got baseball completely out of my system by the time I left for high school. Kareem Abdul-Jabbar always dreamed of the baseball career he never had, and Michael Jordan left basketball to start one. That's not for me. I caused a lot of pain to a lot of baseballs, but when the balls started to get even, I decided to hang it up.

My brothers introduced me to basketball. In fact, my brother Lee used to torment me on court all the time. "I'll let you shoot this time," he'd promise. But just when I got the ball up to the rim, he'd swat it away.

"It's not fair," I'd wail. I'd storm off for home, frustrated and angry. He was a giant, and I was just a little kid.

My best friend, Ricky, had an elite outdoor suede basketball that everyone wanted. I'll never forget that incredible ball. It smelled of rich leather and felt like the fuzz on the perfect peach. That was the ball we always took down to the park. But if Ricky was in a close game, he would suddenly grab his ball and go home. It always happened with the score tied at fifteen when we were playing to sixteen. If he didn't get a foul in his favor, everyone knew what was coming.

"I'm going home," he'd say as he stomped away with that awesome ball tucked under his arm.

We always went next door to Mrs. Brannon's basket when we couldn't go to the park. Her son, Michael, told us about his high school coach, Coach Gray, the winningest coach in the state of Oregon. I was amazed when he talked about this legend as a personal friend.

Then one day, when I was a fifteen-year-old sophomore at Benson High, Dick Gray himself noticed me. He came up to me after a game and laid his hand briefly on my shoulder. "You stick with it. You might have some potential," he said.

To a frail, insecure, fifteen-year-old, this was the best news in the world! From then on, I wanted to please Coach Gray. I was desperate to make the varsity basketball squad. I wanted to learn, to excel, to become a champion. I had a goal to make the varsity team, to play Coach Gray's kind of game, to learn from him. I had found a leader.

I was a common sight my first year at Benson—a 5'10" freshman who played basketball in the neighborhood. I returned for my second year a different person. That summer I had needed a cast on my leg because I had a problem with my joints growing too fast. My brothers had always been taller. When I started my sophomore year, I matched Steve at 6'3". By my junior year I was Lee's height, 6'7", and had learned to watch my head going through doorways. When I got to college, I was 6'8-1/2" and grew to just over 6'9" after I joined the NBA.

In my junior year, the varsity basketball

team was really coming together, but arch-rival Grant beat us in the play-offs, so we didn't make it to the sixteen-team state tournament. Benson's rivalry with Grant is a Portland tradition. When we played, it was almost for blood.

In my senior year Coach Gray started us right off toward a championship season. "If you run the ball, no one can beat you," he told us. We practiced a little defense, and he taught us some good moves, but mostly we just aimed to outscore other teams.

I was the center, wearing number forty-five, and my role was not to score but to rebound. Even so, I was usually double- or triple-teamed whenever I got the ball. They wouldn't play me one-on-one.

"The only points you're going to score are off the offensive boards," Coach Gray said, forcing me to work on rebounds. Every night after practice, assistant coach Pennington drilled me on rebounds, rebounds, rebounds.

When we came up against arch-rival Grant, the gym was packed, including the aisles. No one could move except vertically.

We led Grant from the start. We were up by ten when I stole the ball from an opponent at about three-quarters of the court. I dribbled the breakaway from the outside and drove toward the basket. On the opposite side, a would-be Grant hero was angling to cut me off. I got to the top of the key, and he cut me off five feet from the bucket. During the drive I made up my mind that if I could get the ball near the paint, I was going to dunk it. My teammate Greg West, at just 5'8", could also dunk the ball. But this was my turn.

I dribbled once more, then palmed the ball with my right hand the way I used to see Dr. J. do it on television. The defender stayed with me, jumping in front of me to block my shot. When he sprang up, our bodies collided, but I reached over him and dunked the ball on the way back down. Then I turned and ran back up the court. I ran right into my teammates, who hugged me and slapped high fives.

We beat Grant and rolled the rest of the year. In the play-offs we killed Grant in the first round. Then we won every game in the state tournament, taking us to just one win from the championship. We were favored to win, but the challenger for our last and final game was number two, Hillsboro. Whoever won the game took home the state championship and a lot of pride.

When the game started, I got two early buckets, and we were up 10–4 in three minutes. That forced them to run, to play our game. We

A.C. Green

were up by ten at halftime and stayed pretty much in control of the game from then on. With 2:56 left in the final quarter, we led by fourteen points.

"We're number one! We're number one!" the Benson crowd chanted.

But within forty-five seconds of that fourteen-point lead, Hillsboro had cut it to seven. Suddenly, our team was scared. We lost the edge. We lost our concentration. And we were tired.

"Suck it up!" Coach Gray screamed over the ruckus.

With one and a half minutes to play, Sam Morton raced in for a breakaway. We were up by ten. But it wasn't enough. With a minute left to play, we were only ahead by six. They scored, and we were up by four. Greg "Doc" West dunked one to put us up by six again. Then Greg got fouled.

Greg made the free throw that put us up by seven. The crowd started to chant.

"Ten, nine, eight. . . ."

Dean Derrah hit a shot from the baseline, another Hillsboro player scored, and suddenly we were only up by three points.

"Seven, six, five, four. . . ."

John Immel stole the ball from us and

scored again, bringing Hillsboro within one point.

"Three, two, one!"

Somehow the clock ran out, and we squeaked past them 74–73.

"We're number one," I screamed, and then I scrambled to find my family. I looked frantically around until, suddenly, big arms grabbed me, my legs came off the ground, and I was aloft on the shoulders of my brothers and friends.

"We won!" my brother Lee hollered. "A.C., you did it!"

I was on top of the world. My team—Benson Polytechnic—had won the state championship.

4

Heaven or Hell?

Growing up, I attended church and Sunday school just because my parents asked me to. We all went together to Albina Pentecostal Church of God, with Pastor Samuel Irving. But inwardly I didn't understand the need for church. I went through the motions. Once my parents stopped insisting, I stopped attending.

Then, the summer before college, nine good friends asked me to join them on a weekend visit to Hermiston, Oregon, to see one of our old Benson teachers, Rod Bragato, and his wife, Karen. I knew they were with the Fellowship of Christian Athletes, but that was okay.

The weekend went fine. Rod and Karen asked us to attend church with them on Sunday morning. It was business as usual at church until the preacher got up and gave a sermon titled "Do you want to go to heaven, or do you want to go to hell?" I got very uncomfortable. The message was certainly not unique, but the timing was perfect.

I had heard such a message before, but on that day my eyes were suddenly opened to my need of a personal relationship with Jesus Christ. When the pastor asked for people to get straight with God, I wanted to sprint down the aisle, but something stopped me.

"Let someone else go first," a voice inside said. Again I felt the urge, but again I stopped. "They're going to laugh at you if you go first," the inner voice said.

Ricky Stewart was standing right next to me, between me and the aisle. I was waiting for him to go first, hoping he'd make a move, but he didn't budge. Finally, I thrust my way past Ricky and into the aisle.

I was the only guy down there. The pastor looked at me kindly. "Do you know what you are doing, son?" he asked.

"No, I don't," I answered honestly. The

pastor came down and talked and prayed with me while I stood with my back to the audience.

"You may turn around now and face the congregation," he finally said.

Once again, the voices started in.

"All your friends are going to be laughing at you."

"They're going to call you stupid."

"You're not one of the homeboys anymore."

I obeyed the pastor and turned around, and, to my amazement, everyone was smiling at me. They started clapping, high-fiving, and saying, "Yeah, way to go."

In that instant I realized that the internal voices were lying spirits. I had a real enemy I hadn't even met yet who would do anything to keep me from believing the truth about God and myself.

A.C. Green

5

Pressing On

During my senior year I started to attract the attention of big regional schools: the University of Washington, University of Utah, and Oregon State. Most recruiting was done over the phone or with Dick Gray, who screened everyone.

Deciding which college to attend was one of the biggest decisions I ever made. Athletes have to sign a letter of intent by the day they are legally allowed to declare, usually sometime during their senior year. After a lot of painful thinking, I decided on Oregon State. It was only an hour and a half away, and they had a champion basketball program.

The fall of 1981, Lee Johnson and I got to the campus early to get oriented. His brother, Jay, had been at OSU for two years and became our guide.

"Let's go play some hoops," I said.

"Okay, there's only one place to play," he said, "and that's Dixon, where most of the team probably is anyway."

We walked straight across campus to Dixon. Jay opened the door to a two-story, red brick building behind the baseball field. We walked into the bottom level and saw three full-length basketball courts. Two were in motion with the jumps, squeaks, thumps, thuds, yells, and grunts of basketball players.

I stood there, my mouth open. Here were the guys I'd watched on TV: William Brew, Lester Conner, Charlie Sitton, and Danny Evans.

"Here we are, fellas," Jay said, gleaming.

"You," one of the younger players called to me. "Are you playing?"

The only way to stay on the court in pickup games is to win each time, so senior players always teamed up to keep playing. I was on a team with younger players, some of them freshmen like me.

A.C. Green

Boom! A pass found the side of my head. *Whack!* An elbow found my ribs. This was a different game, the real deal. I tried the moves that every freshman's adrenaline says to try. I used my high school layup move that used to fake everyone out. I drove up to the right side of the basket, and when the defender jumped to try to block the shot, I brought the ball down, under my chest, and reversed the layup to the other side of the basket. That move works in high school. *Ka-boom!* The ball was swatted from the other side by another defender.

"Get that garbage outta here," Charlie Sitton said, running back down the court.

I went up for a rebound and got knocked down.

"You better pump some iron," Lester Conner said.

I was nervous. *This is not high school,* I thought. *This is college ball.*

"Don't be coming in here with that weak junk," William Brew said after another ill-fated attempt to score.

"You're too weak, young boy," Danny Evans said as he muscled another rebound.

Mercifully, the game came to an end. "Who are the next losers?" one of the seniors challenged boastfully. "We need some fresh meat."

The older guys never let up, and I kept playing, but I struggled for every point. Lee and Jay joined the game eventually. The other freshmen were trying to dunk, but nothing worked.

For the next few weeks I thought I had missed the bus to the school where I was supposed to be. These guys were monsters. But pressing on was the only way to achieve my goals.

I soon learned that I had to press on, not only in basketball, but in academics as well. I didn't want to do college the jock way. If I was there to learn, I would learn. But academics were not my strong suit. I needed help. So I went to see Tootie Systrup.

Tootie Systrup worked in administration at OSU. She had worked with other athletes and saw them come and go, many of them doing their four-year degree on a six-year plan. Tootie became my tutor, my counselor, my academic coach.

"So you want to graduate?" she said, looking down her nose at me my freshman year as if she were inspecting to see if I had brushed my teeth.

"Yes, ma'am, I do," I said.

"But you don't like school much?"

"No, ma'am, I don't," I said.

"Okay, then take these courses," she said, and she started scribbling on my scheduling form.

Every semester I was in her office, figuring out my schedule, doing what she told me to do.

"If you want to graduate as you say you do, you'd better go to summer school," she said.

Summer school! She was determined to see me graduate. She had the bigger picture for me academically. I went to summer school.

"It's time to declare your major," Tootie told me one year. "Have you decided what you want to do with your life?"

"I know I like basketball," I said.

"Keep going," she said.

"Well, I think I could be a good broadcaster," I said. "Plus I want to tell people about Jesus. I really need to learn how to speak publicly."

"Okay, let's see here," she said, looking over my transcripts and the course catalog. "You could major in speech communications."

"Great!" I said, and it was settled.

Three months later I was in her office again. "So, Junior, you failed sociology," she said. "What happened? Did you turn in your work?"

"I turned in all kinds of papers," I said, "but the professor was less interested in my papers than I was in his class."

"And you barely passed biology. You know what this means?" she asked.

"Summer school?"

"Take these classes," she said, shoving my second summer-school schedule across the desk to me.

With Tootie's coaching I got my degree in four years.

6

Getting Focused

One day in November, during my freshman year, Ricky Stewart called from the University of Oregon, where he was attending. He sounded as if he had just finished running back-to-back marathons.

"There's this guy," he said, "Greg Ball. He prayed with me at a revival here, and I'm a Christian now. You've got to meet him."

A few weeks later I passed some guy on campus and sort of looked at him because he was looking at me. I was just a few steps past him when he spun around and caught up to me.

"Hi, I'm Greg Ball," he said. "Want to come to a meeting we're having here on campus?"

"Sure," I agreed.

That Tuesday I went to his small meeting. Afterwards, a group of us hung around talking. I found out Greg loved sports too. In fact, he was into kick boxing!

During our conversation, I decided I wanted to be serious about God. "I'd like to know Jesus the way you do," I told Greg. "I need to get focused."

"Okay, let's pray," he said in a flash.

People were milling around, but Greg thought nothing of putting his hand on my shoulder and praying out loud for the power of God to be active in my life.

When he prayed I felt a power surge. I had never experienced anything like that before. It's one thing to know you're saved, but another to know the power of God living inside you. I was so excited!

I had been baptized as a kid, but now I wanted to get baptized again, only this time with understanding. On a chilly November morning two days later, Greg, along with Dave Elian, baptized me in the school swimming pool.

"Man, where are you going?" Lee asked me when I headed outside with a towel at 6:00 A.M.

"I'm going to get baptized," I said.

"You're crazy, man," he said.

I started going to Greg's revival every night, and I nailed Lee with it every day. "Lee, guess what happened today! You're missing out, man!"

Finally he said, "Yeah, okay, I'll come in about a week." Two nights later, Lee and two friends, Mike and Clark, went with me. Lee surrendered his life to Christ. Mike and Clark never did. The small group of us who got saved became a Bible study group, which then turned into a church.

Pastor Dave Elian taught me a lot about the Word and building character. He also taught us about the importance of daily Bible reading and prayer. Sometimes he challenged everyone in the church to pray for thirty minutes every day that week. Lee and I followed that to the letter of the law. We sat in our bunks, trying to fill our thirty minutes with one eye closed and one eye on the clock.

"Lee, how much time have we got left?"

"Ten more minutes."

"I don't know what else to pray about."

"Pray about that test coming up."

"Oh yeah, good idea. . . . Lee, how much time have we got?"

God honored our obedience to our pastor,

even though our approach was all wrong. It was a spiritual stepping-stone for us.

Pastor Dave and Greg both encouraged us to go out and witness, to open-air preach right on campus. One day, Pastor Dave, Roger, Lee, and I headed for the quad, the open area where students milled, ate lunch, read, and talked.

"Man, my knees are knocking," I told Roger as we stood off to the side.

"Don't worry," he said. "Just watch what I do."

Dave finished his sermonette and introduced Roger. Roger gave his testimony, read some Scripture verses, then introduced me. I walked forward and stood there.

What am I doing here? I thought. I looked like a fish in a fishbowl, with big, bulging eyes staring at the people milling around. Only twenty people were actually listening, waiting for me to say something.

"I'm A.C. Green," I started. Duh. "And I'm a Christian." I gave my testimony, and one of the other guys wrapped it up. That was the first time people on campus knew I was a Christian. I was no longer A.C. the basketball player; I was A.C. the Christian.

The choice I made to follow Jesus meant I had to be a solid, focused person. I don't focus

on others who might distract me or pull me down. Just because others are doing it doesn't make it right or mean I need to get involved. Likewise, on the court I keep my eye and my mind on the ball.

College was important spiritually because it was there I decided not to be a closet Christian. The Bible says that when you do something, do it with all your might for God's glory. That kind of winning attitude is important to cultivate. Think championship. Think victory.

7

Drafted!

Our team won the Pac–10 conference title my first year, 1982. When the regular season ended, we went into the National Collegiate Athletic Association tournament as the number-four team in the nation. Coach Miller said we were the best defensive team he had ever coached, which for him was saying a lot. In the tournament we tromped Pepperdine 70–51, rolled past Idaho 60–42, then were served our heads on a platter by Georgetown, losing 45–69.

In 1983 we had an adjustment year, changing our game because of the loss of the previous year's seniors. We were still competitive but didn't win the Pac–10 crown.

In the race for the 1984 Pac–10 championship, we pulled even with the University of Washington Huskies by defeating them 64–52 in front of a sellout home crowd.

We played the Washington State Cougars in one of our last games of the season and won 66–55. Then we went to Arizona State to keep alive the drive for our Pac–10 title.

I was rested and ready for that game. All day I bugged my teammates. "Let's get this thing going!" I said.

We went out and ripped the Sun Devils 69–58, our sixth victory in a row. A couple of days later I was named Pac–10 player of the year. I was fourth in the nation in field-goal percentage at .667, and I topped OSU with a 17.5 scoring average and 8.5 rebounds.

Washington State had already won its final game, so we had to beat UCLA on its home court. The game went down to the wire, but we outlasted the Bruins 70–65, which meant we shared the PAC–10 title with Washington State.

In my senior year we went on to the NCAA tournament and played Notre Dame. They beat us 79–70. It was the last NCAA tournament

A.C. Green

game ever played on a home court. Ever since, they've been played in neutral facilities.

One day in my junior year, I was packing up books into my backpack, getting ready to hit the library. "Okay, man, it's that time," Lee said from his perch on the couch. "Where are you going?"

"The library," I answered.

"How about the Lakers?"

"How about them?" I said.

"They're only the best team in basketball," Lee said. "That's who you ought to play for."

"Yeah, right," I said, then headed off for the library. That season the Lakers toppled the Celtic dynasty in the NBA finals. Not only did they crush them, but they did it in Boston, on the Celtics' own court.

As the Lakers heated up, so did my mind. I started seeing the bigger picture myself, watching older teammates drafted to play professionally, catching on that you could get paid for it— a lot! But was it right for me? I prayed seriously for what God wanted me to do.

Lee had decided to go to law school in Texas, where Greg Ball lived. Now he was concerned about my decision. Roger LaVasa shared his concern.

"What about AIA?" he asked one day. Athletes in Action is a Christian basketball team that tours the country, and the players give high school kids and adults their testimonies.

"I'm thinking about that," I said.

"Or the NBA?" Roger asked.

"Yeah, or quitting," I said.

"I can't see God bringing you this far just so you'll quit," Roger said.

"I can't either, but I have to be willing if that's what He wants."

"That's not what He wants," Lee insisted.

"But I'm willing," I said.

I finally gave God my request: I wanted to serve Him. That's all. When I prayed, however, nothing happened. No bells, whistles, or lights. However, I began to feel that quitting wasn't an option. In time I felt that AIA wasn't either.

"Lee," I said one morning after my devotions, "I'm going with the NBA."

"Man, that's great! But you could get drafted anywhere."

"I know," I said.

As I contemplated the draft, I asked my friends to pray for just two things: that I could go to a team in a city that had a good church like ours and that, if possible, I could stay on the West Coast.

My college season ended, and I waited.

I was referred to a local sports representative who helped introduce me to the NBA. He arranged interviews with teams that flew me all over the country.

One interview was back east with some gentlemen I was to meet for the first time. A team assistant picked me up. He took me to a posh hotel and up to the suite the team had rented. When we walked in, I had to adjust my eyes because it was so dark. The curtains were drawn shut. I was introduced and shook the general manager's hand.

He motioned toward a table in the shadows, which I assumed was arranged with the usual spread of food. But as my eyes adjusted, I saw it wasn't food at all. The entire table was full of every kind of liquor imaginable. Then I realized they were trying to test me! I almost laughed out loud.

"Could we get you something to drink?" the general manager asked, lifting his glass toward me as if in a toast.

"No, thanks, I'm not thirsty."

"How do you like our city?" he asked.

"So far, so good," I said. "The ride from the airport looked nice. But the weather's a little brisk."

"And our team?"

"They're great, competitive."

"Well, I'm sure you would fit in here," he said. "Can you imagine yourself playing here?"

"I guess I could," I answered.

"Your college team structure kept you inside the key most of the time," he said. "It leaves some questions about your shooting from the outside."

"I'm very confident that I can stick it from the outside," I responded.

"You would have a good position with us," he said. "You would be quite an acquisition for us."

"Thank you, sir," I said.

"You've had quite a colorful career."

"Yes, sir."

"You've been involved in some extracurricular activities, too, I see. Preaching on campus and fighting pornography."

"Yes, sir," I said.

"Now you know that in the NBA you might hear players talk about their girlfriends. Can you handle locker-room talk?"

"Yes, sir," I said, thinking, *What does he think I've been doing for eight years? Locker-room talk started on the playground!*

"People in the NBA might not have the same values as you. Will that be a problem?"

"No, sir," I said.

"We'd really like to have you," he said.

"Thank you, sir," I said.

I was glad when I felt the wheels of the plane fold up under me as I flew out of that city.

While I didn't appreciate his stereotype of a Christian, I understood that the man's concerns about my playing ability were genuine. The intensity of the pro game is incredible. Only about 320 players play in the NBA at any given time, and dozens of energetic young legs wash out every year.

On draft day most of the guys who expected to be first-round picks flew to New York to be at the Felt Forum, where the draft was conducted. I agreed to go until I thought better of it. If I was going to have one of the greatest moments of my life, would I really want to go back to a lonely hotel room while my family celebrated without me at home? No way. My representative arranged for my family and the media to watch the draft in the presidential suite of the Jantzen Beach Red Lion Hotel just north of Portland.

My immediate family took time off from work. Along with Pastor and Mrs. Irving and Dave and Joan Elian, we drove up to the hotel that morning to await the announcement of my destiny.

At 10:00 A.M. all heads turned to face the television as the draft began.

"Who do you think will choose you?" reporters asked me.

"Oh, I don't know," I answered evasively.

"What team do you want to play for?" they asked. I may have secretly hoped for the Lakers, but I couldn't admit it even to myself. Jerry West, their general manager, impressed me on our first meeting. I felt he was someone I could learn from as well as look up to.

As each draft choice was announced, my heart pounded. The first pick, ninth pick, fifteenth pick, and twentieth pick went by. Each set my pulse racing, and then I'd relax again. But what if I didn't go in the first round after all?

At 11:52 A.M. the twenty-third pick was made. The Lakers announced, "Out of Oregon State, A.C. Green."

I was drafted in the first round. Incredible!

A shriek went up in the room. My family jumped, clapped, hugged, and kept screaming. I covered my face with my hand, feeling almost embarrassed at being so incredibly happy. That's the photo the local newspaper ran.

"How do you feel?" reporters asked.

"I just thank God. I just thank God," I said.

Finally I was able to answer a little more

A.C. Green

clearly. "I want to play the Laker style," I said, "to run the ball, get banged up, and rebound to my heart's content."

My heart was pretty contented right then. Actually it was almost bursting. God had given me all I'd dreamed of and even more.

8

The Lakers

After the draft I went to Los Angeles to meet with the Laker management and negotiate the terms of my contract. While I was there, I checked out a church that Greg Ball helped start. I loved it from the first minute. Both my prayer requests were answered: to be on the West Coast and have a good church to attend.

Los Angeles was a world away from Portland and Oregon State. It was full of fast cars, fast talkers, big money, and even bigger egos. I stopped in L.A., then went straight out to Palm Springs where the Lakers' training camp was held that year.

A.C. Green

On our first night there, we had a team dinner to kick off training camp. I walked into the dimly lit ballroom and saw a single podium and video screen standing in the middle of one wall. A buffet table stretched along the other wall with waiters scurrying around it, bringing on the mountains of food.

The stars gathered in that one room could have taught the least-educated basketball enthusiast a history lesson of the sport. Kareem Abdul-Jabbar is a walking historical monument on his own. By that night, with sixteen years in the league, he had played with, for, or against most of basketball's greats. I heard people at his table call him by his team name, Cap, short for Captain.

I got into the pros just in time to play with Kareem and against another basketball legend, Dr. J., Julius Erving. Kareem presided at Dr. J.'s farewell the next year, and two years after that Doc presided over Kareem's retirement ceremony in Philadelphia. The two were strong competitors. By the time I came along, their competition had turned into friendship, which was interesting because Dr. J. became a Christian, while Kareem turned to Islam. Kareem was serious about his religion, too.

"You should watch these," he told me once

on a road trip, shoving four ninety-minute videos by a Muslim teacher into my hands. "They'll give you a better understanding."

I was willing to view them and discuss them with him, but two days later he approached me. "You have my tapes?" he asked.

"I barely watched part of one," I started to explain.

"I want them back," he said.

He probably would have viewed, digested, and written a forty-page thesis in those two days. That's Kareem.

That night everyone was dressed casually. I learned later that Kareem is always dressed casually. He was especially fond of one pair of jeans that he wore to home games without fail. On the rare times when he dressed up, he still didn't look like a man at the top of his profession.

Kareem was well known for being a proud man with a hungry intellect and a fierce appetite for privacy. But because he elevated the game, he drew crowds from the beginning. I came to know him as an intelligent man who enjoys reading, thinking deeply, analyzing everything—and playing practical jokes.

Jerry West was Kareem's senior by nine years. He left West Virginia to become a Laker in

L.A. He represented the previous generation, the ones who didn't always get the pay or attention but brought basketball into its own, on par with baseball and football. My relationship with Jerry grew throughout the years into a strong friendship based on trust and respect. He's an intensely loyal person who always keeps his cool and is always confident.

Earvin Johnson was another history maker, known to the fans as Magic, but to the team as Buck. Once we became friends, he and I fell into our family names and just called each other Junior. The 1979 NCAA final between Larry Bird's Indiana State and Earvin's Michigan State is still a classic, and it became a pivotal event for basketball as the two big men fought for the title, which Earvin narrowly won. The rivalry between them became legendary, both on and off the court.

Earvin left college after just two years and was drafted by the Lakers for $500,000 per season in 1979, a record-breaking salary during the days when $150,000 was considered high. Two weeks later Bird was drafted by Boston for $600,000. I think it still irritates Earvin that he came in second.

The year before I joined the team, Earvin and Larry met in the off-season and started a friendship that grew stronger every year. The two of them changed the game of basketball, bringing the sport even further into the national spotlight and making it the game we play today. Earvin had already won three championships with the Lakers before I got there (in his rookie year, 1980, then in 1982 and 1985). To this day I've never seen him in flashy jewelry or clothes that proclaim his success. With all he has earned and accomplished, he has always understood relationships and valued them above all else.

Head coach Pat Riley wore his latest championship ring from 1985, when the Lakers beat the Celtics in Boston. That's the ring Jerry West prized even above the one from his 1972 win against the Knicks as a player.

Coach Riley had been a great player himself and a teammate of Jerry West's for a while. He even played against Kareem, starting back in high school. He had coached the Lakers for four years when I got there, taking them to the finals every year and winning the whole show twice. He's a great coach and masterful storyteller. He prides himself on his locker-room talks. With the results he gets, he has every reason to.

Coach Riley's right-hand man, Bill Bertka, was another ring-wearer who would come to remember me as the "one who affects the many." He coached the big men like me, James Worthy, Kareem, and, later, Mychal Thompson. Randy Pfund was a new assistant coach that year, a rookie like me, who came from a basketball family and had impressive high school and college stats of his own. Years later, when the coaching staff was juggled, leaving him on top as head coach, his faithfulness made a deep impression on me.

I took a seat at the table with the rookies and free agents that night in Palm Springs. I was glad when I caught Byron Scott's eye and nodded to him. He came right over to talk a little. We had played each other in college, so there was a connection there that relieved me. He became my first friend on the team, and our friendship continues.

I continued to gaze around the room. I felt as if my eyes were bulging out of my head. There was James Worthy, the same height as Earvin and I, and one of the best small forwards ever to play the game. James became one of my mentors. His style is courageous and brilliant. He is highly intelligent. He reads about twenty-five percent of what Kareem reads, which puts him two notches above the average person.

I spotted the veteran Michael Cooper at the

next table, laughing and swapping off-season stories with some others. But I soon learned that beneath his calm exterior, he was Mr. Nerves. Before a big game, you could just look at him and he'd start sweating. I avoided high-fives with Coop unless I had a towel handy, because he had the wettest palms in basketball.

Coop was a strong competitor. Even from across the room, anyone could see what good shape he was in. He was slender but thick and solid, not skinny. During the off-season he would hone his body into a machine at his home in Albuquerque. Every year when we checked in for training camp, we'd get our preconditioning reports, and his would always come in showing a tiny percentage of body fat, the best on the team.

I recognized Kurt Rambis when he walked in because of his trademark glasses. He wasn't a dirty player, but he did the dirty work on the team. He got the ball out of bounds after an opposing player's basket or after a missed shot and started the fast break going the other way before the ball ever hit the ground.

In that first year the media tried to make a controversy about my being groomed to take Kurt's position. When I took his starting job in my second year, I was still too young and inexperienced in dealing with high-stakes careers and egos to realize fully what was happening. But I did know that I took someone else's job.

"Do you deserve this position?" reporters asked me. "Are you better than Kurt Rambis?"

Kurt turned out to be a much bigger man than all that. "A.C. works hard," he told the press, "and he does what the coaching staff wants. There's nothing personal between me and A.C."

Kurt's fans weren't quite as friendly to me. Every time he came off the bench to play, they roared their enthusiasm. I lived with that for four years, but I appreciated that he was a champion and had earned their respect and admiration.

The evening was warm outside as well as inside, and I was beginning to feel comfortable in my surroundings. Then management left, the players were alone, and Earvin took the podium to host what he called the "Buck-A-Roam Show."

"Okay, now it's time to introduce the rookies and free agents," Earvin said. "When I introduce you one at a time, you come up here," he said, looking at our table. "Then you can sing your school fight song, a Top 10 song, or a rap." The rookie sang or rapped while the veterans kept time, beating tables or singing backup.

None of the rookies had any musical skills what-soever.

"Go sit down!" they yelled. "Get off the stage!"

My eyes got wider with each performance. My anxiety level rose with each new burst of laughter. I wanted to laugh, but inside I knew I was in trouble. Sooner or later I was going to get called.

"And now, fresh from Oregon State University," Earvin finally announced, "it's Mr. A.C. Green."

I started walking stiffly, my legs trying to take me the other way.

"Come on up, A.C., and give us your school fight song," he said.

"I don't know my fight song," I said.

"Come on—you have to know your fight song!" he said.

The other veterans started laughing. I just stood there and shrugged my shoulders.

"Come on, man—hum it or something," he said.

I fumbled around, looking for a way out.

"I only know gospel songs," I said with a grin. "Do you have any requests?"

"Swing Low, Sweet Chariot," James Worthy called out in his deep, James-Earl-Jones voice.

"Clevvverrrr, Clevvverrrrr," the veterans called out.

"Swing low. . . ," I started as soulfully as I could.

The veterans joined in, ". . . sweet chariot, comin' for to carry me hooommmme. . . ."

Buck let me go with everyone laughing harder than ever. I knew right then that they were wondering about me. They had the wrong impression of me at first—but I also had the wrong impression of them.

9

Rookie

The day after the training camp banquet, I sat on a bench in the locker room, looking forward to my first practice. I leaned over to tie my shoes. Out of the corner of my eye, I saw a pair of huge shoes walk right past me. My eyes followed. I wondered who owned those feet.

I pulled back, raised my eyes, and slowly panned up until finally I saw Kareem Abdul-Jabbar's shaved head. *Wow!* I thought. *There's Kareem!* I shouldn't have been surprised. After all, this was his team. But I just couldn't get used to it.

Rookie

Usually veteran players don't speak to rookies, but on that first day Kareem spoke to me: "Rookie, get me some water." Wow.

Soon I found myself playing against someone I used to watch on television, and I'd think, *Man, I remember watching you while I was in college. You did that same move, went for the rebound that same way!*

For a while I fell into the trap that anyone can fall into. I assumed that successful basketball players were also good people. Reality set in within weeks. I know the Bible says a man's heart is evil apart from Christ, yet I was surprised at how wide the gap was between a man's public and private life. Some of my teammates didn't even know who they were. They were shaky and uncertain, and they tried to cover it up with bravado, talent, and talk.

I held them in such high regard that I could have allowed them to influence me. But I didn't. Instead, I looked at the Hero who would never disappoint me—Jesus. He understands that men need heroes. He had His own hero and role model—His Father. Jesus saw His Father's habits and patterns, and He followed them exactly. He set the standard for us to copy.

Now that I was known by the team as a Christian, the oddball in the bunch, I had to prove myself on the court. The guys didn't know how to handle me, didn't expect me to play with the style and intensity that I had. I guess they expected me to have marshmallow elbow pads—and not to play rough enough to put anyone on the floor. I proved them wrong.

In one early game, however, I just about earned the reputation for poor outside shooting they had been ready to hang on me. On my first trip to Portland I was so nervous and excited that I could hardly remember my name. Byron and Earvin tried to calm me down.

"Just get your first bucket," Earvin said. "Once you get that out of the way, you'll be fine."

"But score in our basket," Byron said, laughing. "And don't let the ball hit you in the head while you're looking for your family in the stands."

"Uncle Junior shot a brick!" my nephews chanted after the Portland game. It seemed like nine years before I made my first basket that night. But, as Earvin had said, once I did, the butterflies quieted down, and I was myself again.

Even though I proved my game, in many respects I remained the odd man out throughout my career with the Lakers. Byron and Earvin were the first two teammates who noticeably cleaned up the way they talked around me. Byron respected me because he talked to me more than anyone else, and we had known each other longer, so he knew I was serious. Earvin just has a great deal of respect for the Christian faith. He often asked me to pray for the team.

The team respected me, but they still wanted to live the way they'd always lived. I remember seeing guys talking privately after one game, getting dressed in sportscoats and splashing on cologne. There were enough fumes to choke everyone in the locker room.

"Why are you all dressed up so nice?" I asked someone.

"Oh, well, a couple of us are just going to so-and-so's house," he said. From then on, not telling A.C. about parties became a Laker tradition.

I loved my teammates, but I didn't need their acceptance to play the game or to live happily. I didn't have to try to live on their level to prove anything to them. And I didn't miss out on anything by not going with them. My first year, the Laker press book listed me as a twenty-one-year-old who enjoyed tennis, bowling, baseball, football, and eating frozen yogurt. Yes, frozen yogurt was a major activity for me.

One day during my rookie year I got ready

for practice and walked into the gym before it started. Earvin was always the first guy in the gym. He and Byron Scott, James Worthy, and a few others were sitting around when I walked in—right into a rookie trap.

Buck said, "Hey, A.C., you've got a phone call in the training room."

To get to the training room, you had to walk down a very long hall, hook a left, then another left, and you were there. I guess they thought they could make me late for practice, which is one of the things you can get fined for. I hurried down to the training room.

"Do I have a call?" I asked Gary Vitti, our trainer.

"The phone hasn't rung all morning," he said.

As I quickly walked back, I knew I had to do something. It took about a minute to walk down that hall, so I had time to think it over.

"Rookie, we got you!" one of them shouted.

"Hey, who was on the phone, A.C.?"

Very solemnly and seriously I looked at them, then gazed up toward that lofty ceiling. "It was my Father," I said softly. There were a few seconds of hushed silence.

I brought my head back down slowly,

looked them each in the eyes, and said, "And now He's waiting to talk to you."

They erupted in laughter.

"Hooo, he got us!"

"The rookie got us!"

10

Staying in Shape

My first few months with the Lakers, I still had my college habits, thinking I could get by without sleeping or eating a square meal. It took only one bad experience to figure out the veterans knew their business.

I went to the shoot-around one morning, then stayed busy all day before the game that night, because the next day we were leaving on a ten-day road trip.

I showed up at the game hungry but mentally ready to play. I grabbed dinner out of the vending machines at the Forum—some candy bars and fruit drinks. That was a big mistake. By the end of the first quarter I had the worst side ache I'd ever had, got dehydrated, and fought cramps throughout the game. I was able to play, but only at about fifty percent of my normal energy level. That cured me forever from looking for shortcuts.

Coach Riley's practices were worse than games, and we had a lot more than eighty-two of them during the season. Even though most of my teammates were seasoned veterans, Riley drilled us on techniques and fundamentals every day. The practices were hard, fast, and heavy, and three hours long, but they were like a religion to us.

That year the Lakers were in transition. Instead of using the dominant center position, they changed to a more balanced offensive game that utilized everyone's talents. You could say we were changing from being Kareem's team to becoming Earvin's team. It was the right time. Opponents were figuring out the traditional Laker plays that keyed on Kareem. One or two could even beat us at our own game. Coach Riley led the transition, and both Kareem and Earvin helped. It wasn't until the next year, however, that it really paid off.

My first year I believed we were going to go

all the way. The league had parity at the time, making every team almost as good as the next. But we were at the top in league statistics. We won sixty-two games.

The Houston Rockets met us in the Western conference final, pitting the "Twin Towers" of Hakeem Olajuwon, 6'11", and Ralph Sampson, 7'4", against our single tower, Kareem. Kareem had to work. He had other players to help him, but Kareem expected to defeat those guys himself. He had already scored forty-two points against them earlier that season.

Going into the series, sportswriters and critics were calling Houston "the team that could beat L.A." We won the first game in the Forum comfortably by a score of 119–107. But then they squeaked by us to win the next three games by a total of twenty-eight points. We were soon on our way back to the Forum knowing we needed to win or we'd be out of the play-offs. With thirty-seven seconds left in game five we were still up by three. Then Houston's Robert Reid hit a three-pointer and tied it. We attempted another shot, missed, and they called a time-out with the score tied and two seconds to play.

Time-out ended, and Houston's Rodney McCray took the ball out of bounds right in front of our bench. He lobbed it in to Ralph Sampson.

Sampson caught it about five feet from the basket, with his back to the net and Kareem on him, trying not to foul. A second ticked off by the time he caught it, so he didn't have a chance to dribble, to reset himself, or even to land. We all caught our breath to see what he would do. He sort of twisted in the air and threw it back behind his head with a limp, weak toss that seemed to say he would settle for a tie and overtime.

Was it over? We all watched as the ball hit the front of the rim and rolled slowly to the back. The world was frozen in slow motion for everyone in the Forum. The players were all eyes, watching that slow ball take its time to decide what it would do. The roll to the back brought it to a stop, and it seemed to hang on the back of the rim just for fun, to prolong our pain. After a moment it dropped down, right through the hoop.

The Forum was dead silent. We heard the dull thud of the ball bouncing on the floor beneath the basket.

I hate to lose. I especially hated losing that day. If I'm going to get beaten, then beat me. Don't make me lose because of some lucky shot. I was frustrated, disappointed, and had a lot of work to do on my knees to figure out what God was doing in all of this.

The last thing I expected when I came back the next season was an injury. That's something the average car salesman or manager probably doesn't think about, but it's something professional athletes think about every day. We have to stay healthy and in top condition to compete and win.

To maintain good health, exercise fits alongside a good diet. During the off-season I generally get up before dawn, read my Bible and pray, then stretch and ride my bike the half mile to my neighborhood park. I run three or four miles around the park, then jog to a nearby track, where I run sprints. That keeps my wind ready for the following season. I'll run six or eight hundred-yard dashes, then six or eight fifty-yard dashes. Then I'll go to the gym to lift weights. The point is to have fun while you're staying in shape. Then it won't seem like work.

Your mind has to get in shape, too. Pat Riley had hard practices, but they prepared us well. I call it "toughness with gladness." We forced our minds to control our bodies.

It's the same principle in the kingdom of God. You tell your body to get up and go do something right, and all of a sudden your body starts talking junk to you.

"Oh, no, I want to stay in bed."

"I don't want to go to Bible study."

"No, I don't want to confess my sins."

You have to control your mind and body to make yourself do what you know to be right. Those who accept compromise or want to find the easy way can never perform at the highest level.

We always practiced with more intensity than we had in an actual game. Coach Riley wanted us to react instinctively to game situations. The only way to do that was by practice. Practices prepared us mentally as much as physically to endure to the end, to keep our concentration, to react quickly and instinctively, and to win the game.

Like any athlete I get little injuries. I call them game souvenirs or fender benders. I twist a finger, suffer a knee in the thigh, or get the smile to the back of the head. But I had a serious injury at the beginning of my second year with the Lakers.

We were playing our last preseason game against the Suns. In the second quarter I bent my thumb back. It hurt, but I kept playing. I scored twenty-four points and got thirteen rebounds, and we won.

Before we left, I asked Gary Vitti to tape my thumb, but it kept hurting, even then. We flew

A.C. Green

back to L.A., and I had it checked out thoroughly. I had hyperextended it up and over the back of my knuckles. No wonder it hurt. I had a torn radial collateral ligament that required surgery.

I drove myself to the hospital in L.A. for my second appointment. The next thing I knew, the nurse started preparing my hand for surgery and said I was going to be hospitalized overnight.

"We're going to give you something before the general anesthesia," she said, then pulled out a needle and poked me. "This should make you feel a little drowsy."

The same nurse was on duty when I came to the next morning. "You were out for the whole operation just from that relaxer."

After surgery my hand was put in a huge splint the size of a Ping-Pong paddle. Gary Vitti fitted me with a smaller one that I ended up wearing all season. I missed just three games total, the last one on November 18, 1986, which turned out to be the last game I have ever missed as a professional.

Keeping my body pure from immorality is another part of my overall conditioning. Sex affects every part of life, not just the physical. So when I became a Christian, I made a vow not to be with a woman until I married.

I always have a choice to make. If I'm tempted by some woman or even a TV commercial, I don't have to look. I don't have to treat women like a piece of meat in a shop. It's my choice. I exercise my power of choice to keep control of my own body, my own life. In high school I had relationships with women that never resulted in sex. Most of the guys I hung around with pressured me to have sex to be included with the homeboys. Like a lot of kids I talked a lot, but nothing happened.

When my friends were telling me how much fun I was missing out on, the grace of God kept me. It wasn't that I didn't want to have sex or didn't think about it, but my self-respect never broke down before I got saved, and it strengthened afterward.

The media, athletes, and entertainers scream in word, action, and lifestyle, "The normal, natural way of sex is to have it whenever you want to, but try to do it safe, and don't worry about the consequences." People believe the lies. Condoms are hailed today as the answer to sexually transmitted diseases (STDs) and unwanted pregnancies. The facts are, however, that they fail to prevent pregnancies 15 to 36 percent of the time; they leak the HIV virus, which is said to be 450 times smaller than sperm; and unwed pregnancies have increased among teens 87 percent since the start of the government's birth-control crusade. We'll never stop the AIDS epidemic unless we stop sexual promiscuity, which is the most common way of transmission.

During my sixth year in the NBA, I formed Athletes for Abstinence to teach that the only one hundred percent sure way to avoid STDs, unwanted pregnancies, and AIDS is sexual abstinence. We teach that sex in itself is not wrong and was actually created by God, but that sex outside of marriage is not worth the risks.

Even if you've been sexually active, it's never too late to say no. You might feel guilty or unworthy, but God will forgive you. Abstaining from extramarital sex is one of the most unpopular things a person can do, much less talk about. But it's the best alternative if you want to live a happy, healthy life.

If you can control yourself sexually, you can control yourself. Period.

By my third year in the league, news reporters were calling me a "third-year pro" instead of a "third-year rookie." I felt that part of the test I had passed, in terms of achieving respect, was a moral test.

That year, after a regular-season game

against the Mavericks, Greg Ball was waiting for me as I exited Reunion Arena in Dallas. Usually Earvin was the first one in and the last one out, but on this night he came out right after me. Three ravishingly beautiful young women were waiting for us. They came up to me, smiling and saying cute things to try to strike up a conversation.

"Hey, A.C.," the first one said.

"How are you girls doing?" I asked.

The one in the middle answered, "Fine, now that you're here."

"You know what you girls need to do?" I said. "You need to repent and get real jobs."

Earvin jumped right in. "Yeah, that's right!" he said.

I let them know I wasn't trying to put them down. I just needed to make it clear where I stood. Earvin and the rest of my teammates followed me as I walked away, leaving them behind.

One by one I earned the respect of my teammates. "We've heard rumors," a reporter said to James Worthy one day, "that A.C. preaches too much."

"People respect A.C.," James said. "A lot of guys who joke about him and give him a hard time probably want to be like him but don't think they can."

Even Kareem stood up for me. Once during a shoot-around, one of my teammates was jiving. "I'm a Christian," he said. "I'm just like A.C."

Kareem shut him down fast. "No, you're not even close," he said. "No one else on this team is like A.C."

11

Giving and Receiving

My apartment in L.A. wasn't exactly the kind of place you'd expect for a professional athlete. The nicest things in the apartment were my bed and the television set; otherwise I had a well-worn yellow sofa, mismatched chairs, and orange crates for end tables.

I could have lived well with what I earned, even though my first contract wasn't great. But money was not the object. Deeper things motivated me. I wanted to learn to trust in God to

A.C. Green

meet my needs. And I didn't want to be lured into the fast lane.

When I first moved to L.A., I wondered when I met someone, *Does this person really like me for me? Or does this person want something from me?* The veil of cynicism and mistrust that seems to hang over the L.A. area was trying to envelop me.

My superbrothers came to the rescue— Greg Ball; Phil Bonasso, who was my new pastor; old friend Lee; and new friends Dave Soto and Tom Sirotnak. Greg came out from Texas and spent a lot of time with me. Lee Johnson was in Austin at law school, but I knew he was praying for me.

I asked Dave Soto, who was single, to room with me. People thought it odd that a professional athlete would want to have a roommate, but since I was fighting a desire to be totally independent, I didn't want to be alone. I also needed someone around to hold me accountable. I love myself, but I don't always trust myself. Dave stood with me and believed with me the way Lee had.

I had started financial planning with some experts under Jerry West's careful, brotherly eye. Pastor Phil was teaching us to believe in

God, not just in our own salary. We were trying to look beyond our money to the Maker.

So Dave and I agreed that to learn to live by faith, we would ask God to provide for our needs. Except for our food, gas, and rent, we asked God for the rest—to furnish our apartment and provide us with the things we ordinarily would have bought ourselves.

Our apartment was a running joke at the church. People asked if we were decorating or desecrating. But we won the sympathy of some of the sisters. They brought us needed items or offered to come over and clean. I noticed, however, the same ones never came back to clean a second time.

I soon lived up to the looks of my apartment because I became the lowest-paid starter in the NBA. I could have easily asked for and received more from the Lakers. Instead, I asked God to increase my faith in Him before He increased my salary.

It wasn't too long before that prayer was answered in an unexpected way. After going for months without a VCR, I finally broke down and admitted to Dave that I needed to watch game tapes at home.

Dave said, "Let's pray about it."

"But, Dave, I really need it," I answered.

"Come on, man—–we've got to believe God for everything," he said.

I didn't want to let him down, even though I was hesitant to put God to the test. As I drove to practice the next morning, I gave it to God.

"God, I need a VCR," I said. "I'm going to believe You will provide me with one."

Once said, I felt better about it. The next morning I prayed about it again during my devotions. Then I drove to the Forum, checked my box as usual, and almost started laughing. There in my box was a note from a season-ticket holder named Doug Kanner. It said he wanted to give me a VCR. My faith soared. It was uncanny. I became friends with him and his family after that and always watched for them at games.

God taught me His pattern: "Freely give; freely receive." I love to give and serve others. I love ushering, taking the offering, and helping with the setup and teardown at church. But I had a hard time letting people do things for me. Like a lot of men, I wanted to be strong and independent. But God showed me again and again that it was important to stay connected to Him and His people. I needed to learn to give—*and* to receive.

12

National Champions

The 1986–87 season turned out to be everything God promised. Midway through the year, the Lakers outbid Boston and Houston for Mychal Thompson, a former Portland Trail Blazer whose contract was up for grabs. Mychal added a lot of life to the team. He also added a lot of talent.

The week the Lakers play the Celtics is the biggest in the Laker year, with Laker fans unfurling their colors and some of the enemy's fans venturing out in green "suicide" shirts. The game at home is the players' favorite. The first thing we always checked when we got our schedule at the beginning of the season was when we played the Celtics at home. James Worthy, Mychal, and I rotated during the game, matching up against Kevin McHale, a guy the *Los Angeles Times* had termed "unstoppable." He had many post moves near the basket. He had a turnaround jump shot, a jump hook, a running hook, and all kinds of crazy shots that confused defenders.

Then there was Robert Parish, Boston's center, who could occasionally outrun a small forward down the middle of the court to get a layup. He got a lot of easy buckets that way. He also was an exceptional rebounder and was famous for a high-arching turnaround jump shot. From seventeen feet in the air it dropped down, touching just the net as it swished through.

Boston quickly jumped to a ten-point lead. Earvin's free throws and James's and Mychal's assists helped, but we still trailed by eight at halftime. When we came back after the half, Larry Bird's game was on, and he took the Celtics to a seventeen-point lead.

Earvin wasn't going to be outdone by Larry,

especially at home. Earvin and Mychal both had something to prove, so they picked up their game, scoring fourteen points in five minutes and bringing us within four by the end of the third quarter. In the fourth, Boston held the lead until the final two minutes. Once again it was Earvin and Mychal saying, "Not on our court you don't," and we edged them 106–103.

After big games like that, the coaches always did a team MVP, which Mychal won easily. He had a great game, earning his keep in just one day.

We stayed at the top through the end of the season, then blew through Denver 3–0, Golden State 4–1, and Seattle 4–0 in the play-offs.

We started the finals in the Forum with another star-studded crowd. We smothered Boston in game one. Even after Larry Bird hit his first eleven shots in a row, we won 126–113. Trying to stop us was like trying to stop a class of first-graders going to recess. Coop broke a record by shooting six three-pointers in game two, and the newspapers called him "human fly-paper" on defense. His game helped us rout the Celtics again, 141–122.

But when we got to Boston for game three, we went flat, and they won 109–103. After the game Coach Riley was smoking mad.

A.C. Green

"None of you has given one hundred percent!" he yelled at us in the locker room. "Who can tell me you've given one hundred percent?"

No one said a word. He was right. After two big wins it was hard to stay mentally tough.

Coach Riley's tirade that included me as a target was unusual for him. Usually, Riley would rip everyone apart, sometimes showing guys films of how bad they were. Then he'd wrap it up.

"God bless A.C.," he'd say. Only he'd say it more like, "Gaaawd bless A.C."

"He's the only one," he'd continue, "the only out there who is really working. A.C., do you have something to say to us?"

In school you have teachers' pets. In the NBA you have coaches' sons. They called me Coach Riley's son.

We showed for game four ready to play ball. We tried hard, but the Celtics fought harder, and with two seconds left to play, they were ahead by one. Earvin would get this special look in his eye when he refused to accept defeat. We all knew that look. He wore it the entire second half of that game, and he never let up even when the game looked hopeless.

With two seconds on the clock Coop inbounded the ball with a pass to Earvin. Earvin got the ball, drove across the lane, and threw a

Kareem-style skyhook that none of us had ever seen him shoot before. We stood with our mouths hanging open as it arced toward the bucket. Earvin had his mouth open, too. The shot was good. We won 107–106, leaving us a game away from taking the whole show.

We had a chance to repeat the victory of 1985 by beating the Celtics in Boston in game five. But instead we came out stiff, and they came out fighting to win. Final score: 123–108. Earvin's winning look never left his eye when that game was over. He didn't accept defeat.

We returned to the Forum for game six. Boston led 56–51 at the half. Two minutes into the third quarter James made a play that is still considered one of the NBA's greatest moments. James swatted the ball away from Boston's Kevin McHale and chased it down the sidelines. He dove headlong to keep it in play, shoving it toward Earvin, who was already on the fast break. Earvin took it at a full gallop and dunked it. That gave us the lead, 57–56.

That quarter we played one of our greatest periods ever, outscoring the Celtics 30–12. Kareem had to sit out most of the third and fourth quarters with four fouls, but he still finished with thirty-two points in just twenty-nine minutes of play. James and Mychal took over

A.C. Green

for him, and we didn't skip a beat. The first-graders made it out to recess. We won 106–93. The series and the championship were ours.

"There's no question this is the best team I've played on," Earvin said when it was over. With his fourth professional ring, that was quite a claim. It was also the Lakers' fourth title of the decade. It was my first professional championship.

13

Fight!

About five times a year I manage to get myself in trouble. In my rookie year, Byron and Earvin often coached me to stay calm no matter what came my way.

"Stay cool," Byron would say as he ran past me after I took a knee to the thigh.

"Easy, Junior," Earvin would say when I went to the free-throw line after an elbow caught me. He always sensed when I was about to erupt. "You're okay. Keep your cool."

I learned quickly that as soon as you think about revenge, you start missing rebounds and

A.C. Green

free throws. The other player beats you when he gets your mind on him and off the game.

One game Pat Cummings of the New York Knicks tried to stop my rebounds. He talked trash and pushed me, trying to make me either foul him or fight him. Finally he threw a fist at me, which is supposed to bring an automatic ejection. But the ref didn't see it. Michael Cooper did, however. Coop tackled Cummings, taking out two rows of chairs along the sidelines. They were swinging, and I saw Coop go down under Cummings. I jumped on top and tried to pull Coop out of there. It looked pretty wild to the crowd, especially to Greg Ball who was there that night. The ref threw us all out—Cummings, Coop, and me.

I went back to the locker room with Coop. The emptiness was eerie. Ejections make guys feel stupid, sitting there, watching monitors, seeing what's happening just yards away.

"You looked like WWF wrestlers!" Mychal said when he came in.

"If trouble starts, you have to be there," Coach Riley said. He spoke with great understanding. "You did what you had to do. Fortunately, we won even without you."

"You should have seen it!" Byron said when we left Coach. "Chairs flying, shirts ripping, guys jumping off tables ten feet in the air, the pile of bodies on the floor—what a fight!"

I left the locker room happy to be out of there. I thought the night was behind me. Greg and I got in the car to leave. He was quiet.

"That was different," I said to break the ice.

"Brother," he said, "you can't do that stuff and call yourself a Christian."

"Greg, I was defending my teammate."

"Ace, you've got to watch yourself. People depend on you."

"But you gotta defend yourself when someone attacks you," I insisted.

"You have to defend your witness, too," he said, refusing to back down.

He was partly right, and I shut my mouth. I am a witness for Jesus. But I have to defend my teammates, too. Balancing the two is what makes a wise, mature warrior. Most of the time, though, I walk away from potential fights.

When I play ball, I play aggressively. I get hit. I get thrown nine rows high in the stands. But that's part of the game. Even trash talk has a place in basketball. But I have my rules for trash talk: no swearing, nothing derogatory about an opponent, and nothing about mothers or sisters. And my best trash talk consists of my "secret" lethal weapon—prayer.

A.C. Green

14

Repeat

No team had won back-to-back championships since the Celtics of 1968–69. In 1987 Coach Riley promised that the Lakers would repeat in 1988.

We got to the play-offs with sixty-two wins and twenty losses. We swept San Antonio in the opening series, but we had to fight long and hard to beat Utah and Dallas.

Finally, we squared off against the Detroit Pistons. We hosted Detroit at the Forum in game one because we had the best record. Earvin greeted his friend and rival Isiah with their traditional kiss. Meanwhile, I matched up against a veteran, 6'5" Adrian Dantley, a two-time NBA scoring leader. In game one he scored thirty-four points, probably thirty-two of them against me. His senior moves and mind games took me apart.

We squared off. I was hot, hyped, and ready for him. He dribbled right, then stepped away from me. He started to shoot the ball, so I committed to block the shot, but he drove around me to score.

"Your twin brother would fall for this stuff," I said.

"You can't hold me," he answered. "You can't hold water. You can't hold your own hand."

I was determined to get this guy. The next time we isolated one-on-one, we were about eighteen feet from the basket. Instead of dribbling, he took the ball, looked over me at the basket, crouched and began his spring to shoot right over my head. Pretty gutsy move to go right over the defender.

This ball is not going in, I thought. *I'm going to get this one!*

I sprang up to swat it down. There, from the rafters, I looked down and saw that Adrian's feet had never left the ground. As soon as I was airborne, he drove past the place where I had been

Repeat

standing and made the easy layup. Not even my teammates had time to come to my rescue.

I was skinned alive. We lost by twelve points, and I went to the locker room with my head hanging.

You, A.C., are one of the main reasons we lost this game, I told myself.

My coaches confirmed my thoughts.

"Junior, he was your assignment," Coach Riley said. "You have to find a way to stop him, or I'll find someone who can."

I went home in total misery and defeat. That night I spent a long time in prayer. The next morning I got up ready to fight. I had lost one battle, but I wouldn't lose the war.

"Are you going to stop him today?" Coach Riley asked me before game two.

"I'm going to get him before he gets me, Coach," I said. "I'm gonna stop him."

In game two I kept my word to Coach Riley. Adrian Dantley was a great offensive player, so I made him play defense. I used my size and quickness to beat him. I made him worry every time I got near the ball.

"Just get the rebound, Junior," Earvin said. "Get the rebound, pass it to me, and run as fast as you can."

I fought for those rebounds, passed to

Earvin, and ran to the other end, where he passed and we scored. We held Dantley to nineteen points and won by twelve.

Detroit was Earvin's hometown, so the hoopla was incredible when we moved there for game three. We had to be focused. They had the second largest crowd in play-off history—39,188 fans.

Coach Riley tried to ward off distractions so we would concentrate. He had one of his famous talks with us on Saturday, the day before game three.

"Is there anybody in this room who has made his best effort yet in this series?" he asked. "Well, that's what we need to beat Detroit at home."

Kareem started game three hitting his first two shots. Everyone joined in, and we made our first six. Then we fell flat, going six and a half minutes with only two points.

"Just beat them on the boards," Coach Riley said during a time-out.

"Just shoot," I told my teammates. "If you don't have a good shot, shoot anyway, and I'll get the rebound."

My game was on. They fought back, but we led 47–46 at halftime.

The Pistons had no more thoughts of shutting

us down. Adrian had no more disrespect toward me. In fact, he began to fear me.

Coach Daly came apart. He hated to lose, especially in front of 39,188 fans. In the fourth quarter the Pistons were flat, unable to make a run or score on back-to-back possessions.

With 5:05 left to play, Coach Daly got in referee Earl Strom's face after a battle in the paint. He was ejected, leaving his team not only lost at sea, but also without a helmsman. We held Dantley to fourteen points. Isiah scored twenty-eight, but we won 99–86.

The Piston guards, Isiah Thomas and Joe Dumars, were not going to be denied in front of their own fans. They came out for games four and five like twin tornadoes and won the next two games. We headed back to the Forum for game six. We trailed 3–2 in the series. They only had to win one more.

Each game in the play-offs is like a moment of truth. Once again, the gut check. *Can I defeat this opponent? Am I ready?*

After winning game six, game seven in L.A. was the same old dogfight. Isiah had sprained his ankle in game six, and he was listed as doubtful for game seven. But he still came out like a wounded warrior and fought valiantly.

James Worthy started game seven with six-

A.C. Green

teen points in sixteen minutes, taking us to a 34–28 lead. The Pistons quickly answered with a 16–7 run that put them ahead 42–41. Kareem made a bad pass over Earvin's head. Isiah got the easy layup. We went into the locker room at halftime trailing and feeling pretty bad about eleven turnovers in the first half.

"This is it," we told each other.

"This is what you worked hard for in training camp," Coach Riley told us. "This is what the regular season was all about—getting a chance to win another championship."

The Pistons held their lead for three minutes in the third quarter. Then we made ten shots in a row. James scored seven of the first eight points. Byron scored eight straight points in the quarter. We led 83–73 at the start of the fourth.

Coop took his turn next, scoring one of two three-pointers that brought us to a fifteen-point lead. With 7:30 left to play, out came the "Lakers 1988 NBA Champions" T-shirts.

With a minute and eighteen seconds to play, our fifteen-point lead was cut to two. Earvin made one of two free throws. The Pistons' Bill Laimbeer missed a three-pointer. Dennis Rodman missed a jumper. Byron was fouled and made his free throws. Tension rose on the sidelines. A four-point lead is nothing in the NBA.

Bill Laimbeer hit a three-pointer to bring them within one point. With seconds left to play, we led 106–105. They could still win.

I'll never forget those last six seconds. Earvin got the ball. He saw me run downcourt, and he faked a lunge, then stopped, pulled back, and passed a seventy-foot lob to me.

Suddenly I was confused. I wondered, *Are we up by one, or do we trail by one?* I drove to the basket with Bill Laimbeer breathing down my back. I didn't want to shoot that ball. *Is everyone depending on me, or can I just run out the clock?* I thought in a panic.

Then I got a surge of courage. "It never hurts to score," Dad always said.

I went up awkwardly. And I scored.

We won by three points.

Twenty years earlier the Celtics had claimed their second straight championship in the Forum, winning 108–106. Now we had done it 108–105.

We walked down the ramp into blinding camera flashes and television lights. As we ran into the locker room, reporters pressed against us. "A.C.," one of them asked me, "is this the greatest moment of your life?"

"No," I said. "Getting saved was."

15

Teammates

In basketball, like a lot of other team sports, you can't play for yourself. You have to play to win. Some players watch their stats because they get paid for their numbers. But ultimately they get paid to win, not to rack up stats.

To win a game you have to know your teammates and become a team player. When I join any team, my primary goal is to glorify God, and my primary mission field is that team. They're my extended family.

Earvin was one of my best friends on the

team. He was the kind of team player who earned the right to be called Magic. On the court he was a naturally talented, intelligent, and unselfish player. Off court he was outgoing, the life of the party, the captain of every ship. He loved being part of a team. On the road he loved people, and he never tired of signing autographs.

"You go over there and sit," we told him at airports before they started chartering flights for us. "The crowd wants your autograph, Buck, so get them away from us."

"You're just jealous," he said, laughing.

Kareem was another team player who became a good friend. He is still considered by many to be the greatest basketball player.

Kareem was usually a gentle giant. He was gracious and generally soft-spoken. But when he got riled, that giant would awaken, and he would yell long and loud. I loved bringing out that side of him. He was usually so cool, so nonchalantly perfect in his play, that I got a kick out of upsetting him.

In my rookie year, when I was still trying to figure Kareem out, I elbowed him or pushed him at practice.

"Sorry," I said.

"Okay," he said the first time or two.

I kept pestering him. I stepped on his foot, tripped him, pushed him off balance. When he finally got upset, his face didn't express anger—his whole body did. His famous goggles would start to cloud. He did deep neck bends, and his ropey arms would swing. He ran down the court, head bobbing, arms cutting huge arcs, goggles steamed, and we knew the next person who defended him was going to get smashed.

"Your turn to guard him," I would tell some unsuspecting teammate. Then I'd watch, laughing, as Kareem gave him the business.

Sometimes you get thrown together with people you don't think you'll get along with, especially in a small church, school, office, or basketball team. But if you chip away at the surface, you may find a diamond in there.

Vlade Divac, a 7'1" center from Yugoslavia, joined the Lakers during the 1989 season. I knew he had joined but hadn't met him officially. Then one day I was in Marina del Rey with my friend Kerry Jones, getting a frozen yogurt. I came out of the store just as Vlade came out of a store across a broad parking lot.

"Look at that seven-footer," I told Kerry.

"Wow, he's tall," Kerry said.

"Hey," I said, "that's Vlade! Let's go meet him."

When we got to him, he was walking around, looking inside a car. "Hey," I called out.

He looked up, and his eyes brightened like a kid's.

"A.C.," he said with his thick, funny accent, and he thrust out his hand to shake mine. "A.C.!"

"How are you doing?" I asked.

"How you do, how you do," he answered.

Then I saw the bent coat hanger in his hand and realized he had locked his keys in the car. "I'll call a locksmith," I told him.

"Yah," he said as he kept wiggling the coat hanger in the window.

Kerry and I bailed him out, but that wasn't the last time Vlade needed bailing. I ended up becoming his American big brother.

"What is wrong with you?" James asked him one day as he strolled in ten minutes late for practice. "Why are you always late?"

Vlade just smiled, his eyes crinkling with sleep in them, his hair sticking out in every direction. "Sorry I late," he said. "I oversleep."

Vlade overslept a lot. It seemed he never got up in time to catch the team bus or get to practice. He was incredibly talented, though, and very funny. I always asked him to translate things for me into Croatian or Spanish.

"How do I say that rookie is a big moonhead in Croatian?" I asked him.

"Neblo glavenya," he said, or something like that.

Vlade was a great addition to the team and an interesting character, but no one was as big a cultural experience as our center from the Bahamas. When Mychal Thompson came during the 1987 season, he quickly took the prize as the biggest mouth in L.A., if not in the universe.

"I've done everything" was his attitude, "and not only have I done it, but I've excelled at it."

"The only team you couldn't beat back in college was mine," he told Earvin in his thick Bahamian accent. Then he went off on something else.

"I only shot in the seventies yesterday in golf," he said. "I shot a couple over par, a seventy-two, with three or four birdies."

"Mychal," someone said, "that doesn't even add up."

"Come to Nassau," he said. He always invited us to his home. "Everybody knows me there. I'll show you the sharks, real sharks, baby sharks, killer sharks."

"Mychal," we asked, "how do you know where to find these sharks?"

"I fight them," he said. "I jump off my surf-board, I go down, and I start kicking at this thing. It's a shark, at least sixteen feet long."

Coach Riley and Earvin took him up on the invitation to Nassau one summer, and one thing was true—everyone there really did know him.

At the end of the 1988–89 season, Kareem retired and left a huge, gaping hole in what used to be the image of basketball. People loved him. Regardless of how he'd treated fans for twenty years, huge crowds came out to see him to the end.

After a 57–25 season, we blew through the play-offs. We broke records by winning eleven straight postseason games, three to get past Portland, four to stop Seattle, and four to rout Phoenix. People started saying "three-peat" about us. We were certain we'd send Cap off with another championship ring. But just before we started the finals against the Detroit Pistons, Byron tore a hamstring.

Detroit led the league that year with a 63–19 won-lost record. We met them on their court for game one and lost 109–97. Things went from bad to worse. In game two Earvin tore a hamstring. We lost by just three points. In game three Cap scored twenty-three points and brought us to within four points of a win. In game four James Worthy put down a career-high forty points, but that still wasn't enough to bring us out on top without our two starters. They swept us. We lost game four 105–97 in front of the Forum crowd on the last day Kareem wore a Laker uniform.

We didn't win the finals, but I found great joy that year in finally getting even with Cap. We all went in together to buy him a white Rolls Royce for his retirement—quite a gift for quite a player. We seated him on the court in a rocking chair before we brought it out, then surprised him. A lot of the old Laker players from previous years came. Cap's son, Amir, sang the national anthem. The ceremony was touching, but the best part came later that night.

While Cap did interviews, Buck, Byron, Coop, James, and I sneaked back to the locker room.

"Come on," Buck said. "Someone get the scissors."

"Where are the jeans?" Byron said.

We took scissors from the training room and started cutting out pieces of Cap's precious pair of jeans. "This is for old times' sake, fella," I said as I cut out a big part.

Other players and former players came in

and got a piece of the action. We folded what was left and put the jeans back on the shelf.

Amir had come in at some point and stood horror-stricken next to the door.

"Dad!" he said as Cap came in the door after his last interview. "They cut your pants! They cut your pants!"

"Who cut them, son?" Kareem asked.

"They all did," Amir said, "and so did A.C. I saw him."

I was right around the corner, so I let out my very best Cap impression: "Hee, hee, hee."

Kareem picked up the jeans and saw them cut to shreds. At first I could see he was mad. After all, this was his prized possession. Then he laughed.

We laughed, too, with the sweet satisfaction of getting even. And I'll never forget the ridiculous sight of Cap holding those jeans up in front of him, trying to figure out a way to wear them home.

16

The Magic and Michael Show

In the 1989–90 season the Lakers were hot again. The joke about evangelists is that they blow in, blow up, and blow out. The Lakers did the same, only we were more like a wrecking crew. We arrived in a city one day, practiced if it was early enough, went to a shoot-around the next morning, destroyed the home team that night, then left the following day to destroy the next team on our list.

"I've got the board," I would yell to Earvin. "Just shoot it!"

Earvin would shoot. If he missed, I would get the rebound against the opponent I had worn down. When the opponents changed their defensive strategy, we just read it and adjusted.

"He's mine," Coop would say, racing past Earvin. Earvin would get the ball to him.

"Face!" Coop would say as he dunked it, short for "in your face."

"You can't make them both," an opponent would taunt when Byron took the free-throw line.

"Well?" Byron would answer, running past the guy after sinking both free throws.

We were hot, winning sixty-three games and ending up at the top of the league. I went after the ball like a kid after chocolate chip cookies, ending the season tops on my team in rebounds with 712 and fourth in scoring with a 12.9 average.

"No rebounds, no rings," Coach Riley said more than once during that season. We were headed for another ring.

When we got back from the All-Star break, we rode the wave until we hit the play-offs. Then we were stopped dead in our tracks during the second round by the Phoenix Suns. The Suns beat us by two points on our own court in game one, and that seemed to give them the confidence to get past us. We got caught flat-footed, and lost.

The team was stunned by the loss. Even though we didn't advance, Earvin was named the league MVP that year for the third time. We heard that Michael Jordan was mad that he didn't win the award. Larry Bird's back was beginning to bother him, so the rivalry between Earvin and Larry was gradually shifting to Earvin and Michael.

That summer Coach Riley announced his retirement. In August, Coop announced his plans to retire from the NBA and play in Italy. I rolled through the upheaval, knowing that part of the original team was still intact with Earvin as our leader.

Mike Dunleavy became the new coach. Vlade Divac was now in his second year. James Worthy, Byron Scott, and I were still the "three amigos" on the team. Two more additions, forward Sam Perkins and guard Terry Teagle, rounded out the team. Rookies Tony Smith from Marquette and Elden Campbell from Clemson came on board and ended up on the ride of their lives.

We slugged our way through another year of dogfights. In November we were shaky, but by midseason, when we went out of town, opposing teams' fans cheered us. The same thing was happening to the Chicago Bulls and Michael Jordan, who really came into his own that year. We finished the season in fairly good shape, behind Portland and Chicago, then started blowing through the opposition in the play-offs.

We went to Chicago to play the Bulls in the finals. It was media heaven: Johnson versus Jordan. Two huddles of reporters swamped the two players. None of the rest of us existed.

In the first quarter of game one, Michael Jordan scored fifteen points, but his teammates missed shots, rebounds, and passes. They were nervous. That was good. We took it to them, with James and Sam each scoring fourteen points in the first half. We led 41–34 in the second quarter; then they led 53–51 at the half. We bounced back, and at the start of the fourth quarter we led 75–68. Jordan came out gunning for us, quickly racking up ten points and running up the score to 78–75, their favor.

The fourth quarter was a seesaw fight between battle-weary soldiers. The Bulls led 91–89 with twenty-four seconds to play when Jordan missed a shot. We called a time-out.

When play resumed, Earvin threw the ball in to Sam Perkins, who squared up behind the three-point line and shot a beautiful arc. The ball dropped neatly into the basket and gave us a one-point lead. Jordan brought the ball back to midcourt, but our umbrella defense stopped him, and the ball went out of bounds. Jordan missed again. We rebounded, got fouled, and scored a free throw to win 93–91. One goal was reached. We beat them at home.

Game two was a nightmare. They were mad and came out gunning for us. By halftime they led 48–43 on their way to a 107–86 rout over us.

The highlight of the entire series came in the fourth quarter. After I missed a routine shot, Jordan got the ball, drove to the basket, and leaped to shoot with his right hand. While airborne, he saw Sam Perkins on his right about to block the shot, so he dumped the ball into his left hand, twisted in the air, and scooped the ball into the bucket. It became one of his most famous plays.

Back in the Forum for game three, the fans surprised us by keeping up their enthusiasm even though the Bulls led 48–47 at the half. The rest of the world thought it was "The Magic and Michael Show," but our fans cheered for the entire Laker team. Vlade scored five times on Jordan and brought us to a 67–54 lead in the second half, but the Bulls roared back. With just over a minute left, Sam scored to bring us within one point. Jordan missed, then Vlade hit an awkward three-pointer that gave us a 92–90 lead.

With only ten seconds in the game, we called a time-out. We had a good opportunity to win. Our whole assignment was to keep Jordan from getting the ball. If he got it, we were supposed to double-team him to make him pass it. Sure enough, Jordan got the rebound. We hustled downcourt, but instead of double-teaming him, we allowed him to get a wide-open shot. He pulled up and hit a seventeen-foot jumper to tie the game. We went into overtime injured and tired. The Bulls won 104–96.

In game four we led 28–27 at the end of the first quarter, but we went into halftime trailing 52–44. We were headed for a 1–3 deficit. We left the locker room at halftime ready to get control of the game. We pulled together, then fell behind by fourteen. We geared back up, scoring seven straight points. They came back. We scored five straight points. It was chess, not basketball. We moved; they matched. We moved; check. They never let up. We lost 97–82, the lowest finals score by a Laker team in forty years. "It was a good try, but you guys aren't going to get it this year" was the feeling we got from Forum staff and management.

But there's not a quitting bone in my body.

I felt like David against Goliath. "It isn't over yet," I told the team at practice the day before game five.

Young Tony Smith hit five of six shots. Earvin's game was on, and he racked up a triple double. Elden Campbell scored twenty-one points total. He and I hit our stride in the third quarter and brought the Lakers to a 91–90 lead. With six minutes to play, the Bulls called time. The Laker fans stood and screamed through the entire time-out. We came off the bench, and our rookie Campbell scored again.

The Bulls' Scottie Pippen quickly shot a three-pointer to tie the score at 93. Two more Bull buckets. One more. With three minutes left, they led 99–93. We rushed back with Sam scoring, getting fouled, scoring, and getting fouled again. We trailed just 103–101 with a minute left. We were still in it. Jordan drove for the basket and lured us to him, but he dished the ball out, and they scored. They got the ball and scored again. And suddenly it was over. The Bulls won the game 108–101 and the finals 4–1.

I hate losing.

17

Two Tragedies

Training camps were a little easier under Coach Dunleavy, but I prepared myself as if Coach Riley were there. We fine-tuned our machines, preparing mentally and physically for the long haul. We were ready to lick some opponents when we left for Utah to play a preseason game on October 25.

On the road it was business as usual, with people flocking to Earvin like an assembly line. He was shaking hands, signing autographs, and posing for pictures.

"Okay," we said, "this is it. You gotta go."

The next day Earvin didn't show up for practice because the team doctor called him back home. On November 7 we practiced at Loyola at 9:30 as usual. Again Buck wasn't there.

When we finished about three hours later, one of the coaches came in and said, "Let's go over to the locker room for a meeting—now."

We went to the locker room and sat in our stalls. Instead of the usual joking and horseplay, the team was silent.

"What's going on?" I asked Byron.

He shook his head and sat there quietly. We sat there for almost a half hour before Coach Dunleavy walked in.

"Earvin is retiring," he told us.

I was shocked. *Buck? Why?* But before I could begin to mull it over, he answered my questions.

"Earvin has the HIV virus that causes AIDS."

This was the first time I had heard those words about anyone, anytime, anywhere. The players sat there, stunned. If I hadn't been sitting, I would have fallen over.

"Buck will be here in a few minutes after he talks to management," Coach said. Then he stepped into his office.

No, Lord, no. I started crying. Everyone did. No one hugged. No one talked. No one looked at each other. I got up and began pacing the floor, crying and praying silently.

The locker-room door opened while I was standing next to it. Lon Rosen, Earvin's manager and one of his best friends, swung the door wide. Buck walked in. We caught each other's eyes immediately. He was wearing his look. *I'm going to get the job done,* his eyes said. I hugged him. He hugged me back as though he needed it.

He didn't know what he would be walking into. The whole room was in tears. Each player took turns hugging him, one by one, stifling sobs on his shoulder. His tough posture crumbled, and he cried. It was the first time he had cried since learning the news.

"This is what's happened," he said. Then he explained how he found out about the virus through a routine blood test.

"It's probably best that I don't play the rest of the season with you guys," he said. "I have to deal with my health situation now. I'm going to fight it. I'm going to take care of myself. I'll be strong and overcome it, and then I'll be back."

He walked out of the locker room and went upstairs for the press conference. We just looked at each other, still stunned.

A.C. Green

For hours I drove aimlessly around L.A., crying and praying. *Why did God allow this?* I wondered. *Why?*

I got together with Earvin as soon as I could. He had been on Arsenio Hall's show saying that condoms could have saved him from catching the disease. I knew through my abstinence work that this wasn't true. Abstinence is the only one hundred percent sure way to keep from catching diseases, including AIDS.

I talked with Earvin just because I love him, but I ended up explaining to him the harm his message could bring. Young people could end up in the same situation as he had if they counted on condoms to save them. In his next interview he modified his message. He started telling people that they should not have extramarital sex, but if they did, to use a condom. It isn't the exact message I give, but it was an improvement.

The real tragedy in Earvin's announcement is that people didn't learn from his tragedy. A great man is down. But people continue in the same behavior. And that hurts.

As close as I was to Earvin, there was an even worse setback in my life when my brother Steve nearly died.

On August 1, 1987, Steve came with some

of my cousins and friends to cheer me on at one of my Portland summer league games. The game finished at about 9:00, and I planned to join him for pizza later.

On my way home, I saw the lights of emergency vehicles. Curious, I parked in front of a neighbor's house and walked down the block toward the accident. From the corner I saw my parents' car in a driveway with the doors open like someone had jumped out in a hurry.

That worried me, so I quickened my pace. I could see a crowd of about fifty people at the bottom of the hill. Over the heads of the crowd, I finally spotted Faye and Mom standing near an ambulance. Suddenly I heard a voice. "There goes his brother," it said.

Dad came into view on the opposite side, so I headed his way. Emergency workers were scattered around inside the group of people, working feverishly. That's when I saw Steve. He was covered in blood and belted to a cot.

I walked back to the ambulance, where workers were fastening Steve in for the ride to the hospital. I couldn't even get to him. I put my palms on the window, spread my hands out, and began to pray out loud. Within minutes the ambulance sped off.

I prayed all the way to the hospital. In the

Two Tragedies

waiting room the atmosphere was heavy with gloom and despondency. "How is he?" I asked.

"They're working on him right now," Pastor Irving said. "He's in surgery."

It was a chilly summer night, but I left the hospital and walked the streets, praying hard. Finally I felt as though I had broken through. The Devil's forces were on the run.

"Still waiting for the doctor," Pastor Irving said as I walked into the ward.

In minutes the doctor walked in. "He's going to make it," he said.

A sense of relief flooded the room. And I was overjoyed. Prayer worked!

I went home as often as I could. My cousin regained his health fairly quickly after a severe neck injury. Steve's progress was slower. First I pushed him around in a wheelchair, and then I helped him take walks. I cheered each new step in Steve's progress.

Now I wait for Steve to make a commitment to God. It's a person's whole life that needs healing, not just a body. As long as they're breathing, God can keep working.

A.C. Green

18

Beyond Victory

After a great summer of ministry, family, and friends, I returned to a team I barely knew. The fabric of the Lakers was unraveling.

First Kareem retired, then Coop and Riley left, and then came Earvin's announcement. We barely stumbled through the 1991–92 season.

Earvin retired in February, a week after he played in his last All-Star game. After retiring, Earvin often came to shoot with us before games, to be one of the guys again. At games we'd see him and Coop in the stands together. They were the best fans we could have. I missed them.

We made it to the play-offs, but we lost in the first round in a rematch with the Portland Trail Blazers. For them it was a grudge match, and we didn't have the spirit or concentration to topple them.

The 1992–93 season didn't look to be any better for the Lakers. I felt like a stranger on the team. That year the Bulls pulled a "three-peat" NBA win. Our team was no longer championship material.

God seemed to be urging me to move on. My second four-year contract had expired, so other teams were contacting me. The Phoenix Suns were a natural enemy of the Lakers by then, but they wanted me. After a long, painful decision process, I signed with the Phoenix Suns on September 28, 1993.

Charles Barkley and I were now on the same team. In general we don't see eye-to-eye.

"I am not a role model," he said in the television commercials that helped boost his popularity.

I disagree. When you make it to the front of the pack, you are a leader and a role model. I make my share of mistakes, but I'm not afraid to let others see how I live my life. As much as possible, I try to measure up to the perfection of Christ.

In 1989 I formed the A.C. Green Foundation for Youth to help build confidence and self-esteem in young people. Volunteers and staff help me run a summer basketball camp for kids, take care of earthquake victims, and sponsor the Special Olympics in L.A.

Of course, my first responsibility will always be to my own family. I take care of my parents as much as they will allow me, and I teach kids to honor their parents, too.

After buying Mom a car, I planned a surprise for Dad. At a ceremony to retire my high school jersey, I invited Dad up to the stage. "Dad," I said, "I want to teach these kids a lesson about respecting their parents. Tell me—what kind of car have you always wanted to have?"

Dad drew a blank. "Well, I don't know, Junior," he said.

I shoved the keys into his hand. "Dad, you know what you want," I said. "So just look out those doors at your new car."

Right then the school officials swung open the huge double doors of the gym. Dad turned and saw the car. He grinned, happy as a clam.

Dad treats that car like the biggest baby. He won't take it out too early in the morning or keep it out too late. And he'll never, ever, skid his tires.

Epilogue

Years ago, before I accepted Christ, I thought I was a good guy. I sat in church, did good things, and made fresh resolutions every New Year's Day. But before I met Christ, I was not in the kingdom of light but in the kingdom of darkness. I needed help. I needed Jesus.

If you have never asked Jesus Christ to be your Savior and Lord, you're not even in the game yet. You can read what the Bible says about why and how to do this in John 3:3, 16 and in Romans 10:9–10. To get started, pray this prayer:

God, I want to become a champion, to fulfill my purpose in life. I admit that Jesus Christ is Your Son and that He promised to forgive me if I just ask. Forgive me for sinning, for compromising, for not pursuing a championship level in life. Wipe it out with your superweapon of forgiveness. Please clean my house and move in as Lord. I humble myself and admit that I need Your help to become a true champion in life. Please take me, change my life, and bring me into total victory. Thank You, Lord.

Amen.

A.C. Green

For information about

The A.C. Green Foundation

**Programs for Youth
Athletes for Abstinence**

contact

575 South Figueroa Street
Suite 2000
Los Angeles, CA 90071

1 800 A C YOUTH
213–622–8326

For information about
Champions for Christ

contact

4505 Spicewood Springs Road
Suite 307
Austin, TX 78759

512–338–0433